Thi[nking of you.]

Desiree T.

Message: Very Proud
of You, Receive Gods'
Guidance + Blessings

From: Tia Rosa V.

Date: 6/16/18

Sunshine for Your Soul

Published by Christian Art Publishers,
PO Box 1599, Vereeniging, 1930, RSA

© 2014

First edition 2014

Designed by Christian Art Publishers

Images used under license from Shutterstock.com

Printed in China

ISBN 978-1-4321-0974-5

15   16   17   18   19   20   21   22   23   24   –   12   11   10   9   8   7   6   5   4   3

Sunshine
for Your Soul

Heavenly blessings to warm
your heart and add a
sparkle to your day

CHRISTIAN ART
PUBLISHERS

Remember,

when things go wrong

and in yourself

you don't feel strong:

Your disappointments

are God's appointments

to bring new hope to you,

for He has promised,

"I'll carry you through!"

Let your **blessings** outshine your complaints.

"Let your light

SHINE

before others,

that they may see your

good deeds and glorify your

Father in heaven."

Matt. 5:16

Do not set your **heart** on earthly treasure, for it can disappear as dew before the sun.

Where **the love of God** reigns fear disappears as mist before the sun.

The best
vitamin
for a Christian is

B1

God is not the architect of adversity,

but He uses it to attract our

attention in order to slow us down

in the rat race so that He can

take us on a course of inner-growth,

which will strengthen our

faith in God

and allow us to enjoy
a closer walk with Him.

God is our refuge
and strength,
an ever-present
help in trouble.

Ps. 46:1

It's during times
of calamity
that in the fiery furnace
He molded me
therewith to prepare
a crown of glory
for me to wear
throughout **eternity.**

If you want to enjoy life,
make the best of every moment.
And if there are dark moments
remember, shadows prove
that the sun is shining.

I press on
toward the goal
to win the prize
for which God
has called me.

Phil. 3:14

God will carry you when you cannot carry on anymore.

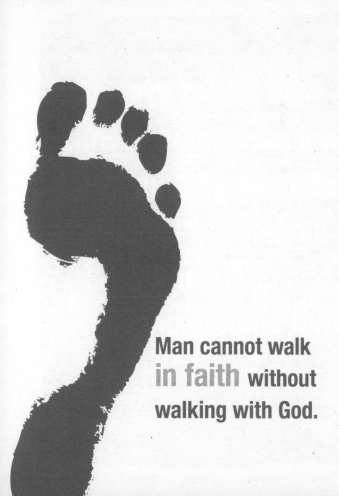

Man cannot walk in faith without walking with God.

We fix our eyes
not on what is seen,
but on what is unseen,
since what is seen
is temporary,
but what is unseen
is eternal.

2 Cor. 4:18

Faith in God
**helps you to
move mountains
of impossibilities
by moving
a stone at a time.**

The hallmark of astuteness

is a person's ability

to forgive himself

as well as others

unconditionally

and to accept God's

forgiveness irrefutably.

The mind is as receptive to thoughts as fertilized soil is to seed. However, as soil doesn't know the difference between weed and flower seed, whatever thoughts you sow **will grow.**

Brethren, whatever things are true,

whatever things are noble,

whatever things are just,

whatever things are pure,

whatever things are lovely,

whatever things are of good report,

if there is any virtue

and if there is anything praiseworthy –

meditate on these things.

Phil. 4:8

Rather be **effective** than active in your work. It's not how much you've done, but what you've accomplished that brings home the bacon.

Life
is God's
gift to be lived
in the present.

In a dark night

you have a choice to say,

"The night is so scary," or,

"The night is
so starry."

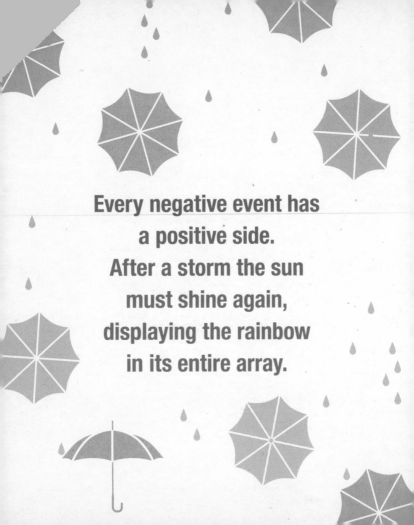

Every negative event has
a positive side.
After a storm the sun
must shine again,
displaying the rainbow
in its entire array.

Always be joyful.
Never stop praying.
Be thankful in all circumstances,
for this is God's will for you who
belong to Christ Jesus.

1 Thess. 5:16-18

It's **amazing** how one possibility-thinking person can speak a future of **hope** in a negative world.

Behind every burnt side is a **bright side** waiting to be discovered.

No matter what happens,
or how bleak things
may be today,
life goes on, and the night
will be followed by a

SUNRISE

and a bright day.

Jesus Christ is the same yesterday, today, and forever.

Heb. 13:8

Hope in man's heart
and the sun shining
in its full glory has
one thing in common –
it **brightens**
a dreary day.

Be glad for shadows –
they are proof that the
sun is shining.

Wrap the whole of your care in a whisper of **prayer**. And God, who is willing to hear, will come, your burden to bear.

**Cast your cares
on the Lord and
He will sustain you.**

Ps. 55:22

God will never leave you nor forsake you. But you have a choice to either turn towards or away from Him in times of trouble.

"Do to others as you would like them to do to you."

Luke 6:31

A person who avoids addressing differences for fear of hurting others is a surgeon allowing a wound to fester for fear of cutting deep to clear the abscess.

A servant of the Lord must not quarrel but must be kind to everyone, be able to teach, and be patient with difficult people. Gently instruct those who oppose the truth. Perhaps God will change those people's hearts, and they will learn the truth.

2 Tim. 2:24-25

you

cannot teach

a chicken-minded person

to fly.

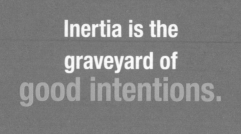

Inertia is the graveyard of good intentions.

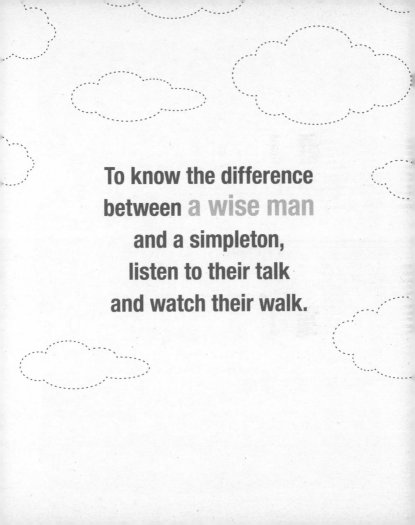

To know the difference between a wise man and a simpleton, listen to their talk and watch their walk.

There is a vast
difference between
those who
know the truth,
those who
love the truth
and those who
live the truth.

A wise man measures his words; a fool keeps on talking without measure.

**The simpleton
parades himself;**
the wise
applauds others.

With God on my side
and within me,
we are a majority,
and with Him
anything
is possible.

Doubt, the absence of

faith,

is like an army

without ammunition –

defeated even

before the battle starts!

May integrity and uprightness protect me, because my

hope, Lord, is in You.

Ps. 25:21

Doubt is invisible, but it calls failure into existence.

Accept responsibility
for your behavior.
If you want to fail,
feed your doubt.
If you want to succeed,
feed your

in God.

Trust in the Lord

with all your heart;
do not depend
on your own understanding.
Seek His will in all you do,
and He will show you
which path to take.

Prov. 3:5-6

If you fail, keep on trying. A battle is not lost until you surrender.

Gain wisdom

**from failures and heartaches
of the past and trust God
to help you to build a
bright future that will last.**

Failure
is not a disgrace –
giving up and
never trying
again is!

Be strong

and do not

give up.

2 Chron. 15:7

The answer to the question, "Where is God when bad things happen to good people?" is, "Right at your side to hold your hand if you want Him to."

Commit everything you do to the Lord. Trust Him, **and He will help you.**

Ps. 37:5

A **positive attitude** and faith in God help to transform crises into opportunities for new beginnings.

Faith
in God,
not w😟rry,
is what takes us through a crisis.

Cast all your
anxiety on Him because
He cares for
you.

1 Pet. 5:7

We were not designed to bear our burdens ourselves. That is why God is there.

You can
exaggerate
mostly anything –
but not the love

of God.

"I have loved you
with an everlasting love;
I have drawn you
with unfailing kindness."

Jer. 31:3

You always have

something to give –

if not from your pocket,

then from

your heart.

I have shown you in every way,
by laboring like this,
that you must support the weak.
And remember the words of the Lord Jesus, that He said,
"It is more blessed to give than to receive."

Acts 20:35

Here on earth we are

in God's school of life.

Let's approach every situation,

good or bad, as an

OPPORTUNITY

to learn from and to excel.

Without the test
of trials there is
no testimony of
grace.

From His abundance
we have all received one
gracious blessing
after another.

John 1:16

You can never fly

as high as an eagle

if you think of

yourself

as a sparrow.

Praise

gives children the wings of an eagle

to reach the heights

they are destined for.

The Lord will work out
His plans for my life –
for Your faithful love,
O Lord, endures forever.

Ps. 138:8

Vision is a picture in your mind

of a better

future.

Motivation, dedication, hard work and perseverance are the wheels of the vehicle that takes you there.

The Lord your God will bless you in all your harvest and in all the work of your hands, and your **joy** will be complete.

Deut. 16:15

Vision **knows**

no boundaries except those
created in your mind.

Vision in the **heart** shines through the **eyes.**

**Be smart of thought
but
humble
in deed.**

Wisdom

is sweet to your soul.
If you find it, you will have
a bright future,
and your hopes
will not be cut short.

Prov. 24:14

The most sincere emotions are many a time expressed in silence.

To make the
best of your life:

Give up the past –

take hold of the present

and build a better

tomorrow.

**Surely Your goodness
and unfailing love
will pursue me
all the days of my life,
and I will live in the house
of the Lord forever.**

Ps. 23:6

The proof of unselfishness is to give the **best** to life, not to get the best out of life.

Do nothing out of selfish ambition or vain conceit. Rather, in humility value others above yourselves, not looking to your own interests but each of you to the interests of the others.

Phil. 2:3-4

Empathy is the spark that ignites understanding of the feelings of people. It is the key to open the door to people's hearts and allow them to share their joys and hurts without the fear of disparagement.

Be devoted to
one another in love.
Honor one another above
yourselves. **Rejoice** with those
who rejoice; mourn with those
who mourn. Live in harmony with
one another. Do not be proud,
but be willing to associate with
people of low position.

Rom. 12:10, 15-16

Empathy builds a bridge of understanding between two people.

Nourish your soul by meditating on godly thoughts, as you would fertilize soil to increase your crop.

Let the words of my mouth and the meditation of my heart be acceptable in Your sight, O Lord, my strength and my Redeemer.

Ps. 19:14

Committing your life
to God's master plan
will turn your life
into a masterpiece.

Commit to the Lord whatever you do, and He will establish **your plans.** Prov. 16:3

The straight and narrow road

is the least preferred,

but it's the only way

to higher ground.

"Small is the gate and narrow the road that leads to life, and only a few find it."

Matt. 7:14

If you put **your trust** in God, He will help you to turn a trial into triumph, victim into victor, test into testimony and a mess into a message.

Since we have been justified through faith, we have peace with God through our Lord Jesus Christ, through whom we have gained access by faith into this grace. Not only so, but we also glory in our sufferings, because we know that suffering produces perseverance; perseverance, character; and character, hope. God's love has been poured out into our hearts through the Holy Spirit, who has been given to us.

Rom. 5:1-5

When someone hurts *you*
and you feel justified
to hold a grudge,

let go

and let God be the judge.

Fill your life with

happiness,

**accomplishment
and distinction by**

believing

**God who loves you
unconditionally.**

Faith in God

produces joy and

peace

even in the midst

of trial and tribulation.

The mind governed by the Spirit is life and peace.

Rom. 8:6

stones.

stepping

into

blocks

stumbling

convert

Winners

You will keep in
perfect peace
those whose minds
are steadfast,
because they trust in You!

Isa. 26:3

Don't put your trust in the wealth of gold, but pin **your hopes** on the living God.

I wait for the Lord,
my whole being waits,
and in His Word
I put my **hope.**

Ps. 130:5

There's more

healing in *silent*

fellowship

than in loud advice.

Start

each day

with a new attitude

and a load of

gratitude.

I will thank the Lord
with all my heart as I meet
with His godly people.
How amazing are
the deeds of the Lord! Ps. 111:1-2

Change your attitude from bitterness to **"betterness"** and you change your mindset from victim to **victor.**

Do everything without grumbling or arguing, so that you may become blameless and pure, "children of God without fault in a warped and crooked generation."

Then you will shine among them like stars in the sky.

Phil. 2:14-15

Your attitude, more than the type of work you do, determines job satisfaction and propels you to excel.

Whatever you do,
work at it with all your heart,
as working for the Lord,
not for human masters,
since you know that you will
receive an inheritance from
the Lord as a reward.
It is the Lord Christ
you are serving.

Col. 3:23-24

It's your choice to start
turning your scars into stars,
pain into gain and
gloom into bloom
by allowing the love of God
to pervade your heart.

Give thanks to the Lord,
for He is good;

His love

endures forever.

Ps. 118:29

I wait quietly
before God, for my
victory comes from Him.
He alone is my rock
and my salvation,
my fortress where I will
never be shaken.

Ps. 62:1-2